NONE OF US

Ted Greenwald
Kyle Schlesinger

kin press

∞

Special thanks to Grant Cross, Chris Martin, and Sarah La Puerta for collaborating on some collages.

∞

Kin Press
P.O. Box 682
Higganum, CT 06441
kinpress.org

Cover & interior design by J.C. Mlozanowski

ISBN: 978-0-9989293-3-0

In the spring of 2016, Ted Greenwald and Kyle Schlesinger began a poetic postcard collaboration comprised of three lines per card. The goal was not to produce a direct call and response, but rather to let the chips fall where they may and arrange the poem chronologically. *None of Us* is not only an exploration of chance and synchronicity, but an experience in free-association and imagined dialogues.

NONE OF US

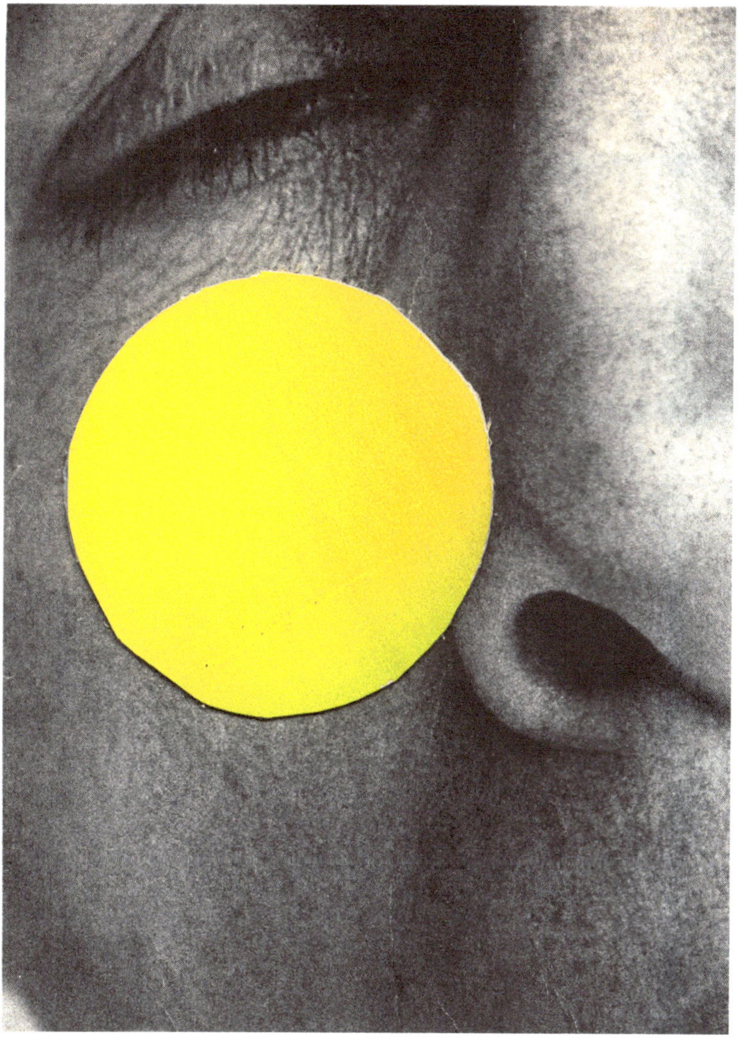

Beam me a zinger
Beautiful beauty parlor
Best backup singers

Bud leaf shadows
Red brick w/ pompom
Window blotters

excuse
me
walk
toward
to
window

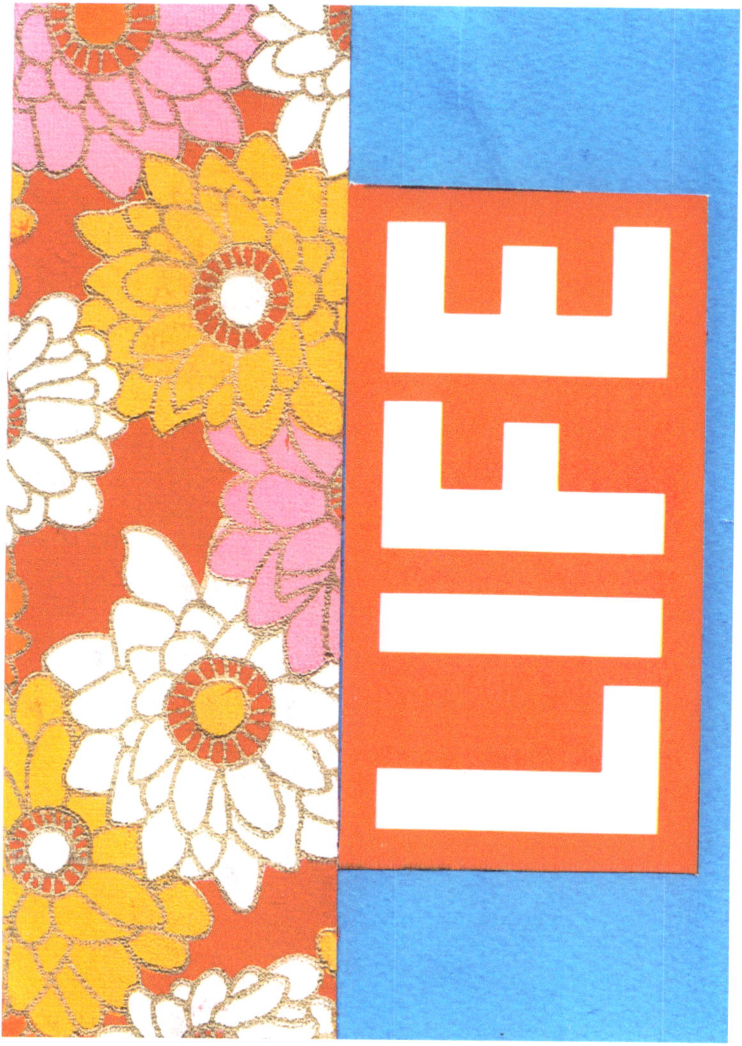
LIFE

Sunset strip
Clams rubbernose
Loosey goosey placebo

Any simple animals
walk by
~~Where is~~ They're people
The very people

gab
bag

come
clean

Matt Dillon hurried over.

With Timmy and several others helping him, the [illegible]hal knelt and put his strong shoulder under

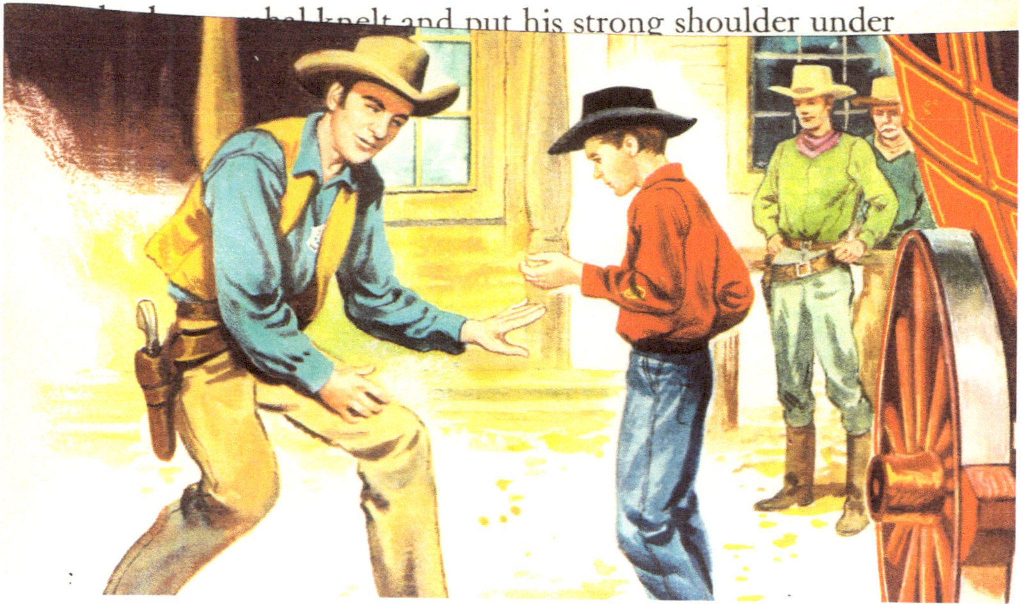

Halcyon days scratch surface
So surmised is a sentence
Angels' braincells

Beyond Sound Bite Valley
Tundra-ing hoofs
Rush hour whistling
snowflakes

Count
on
all
hands

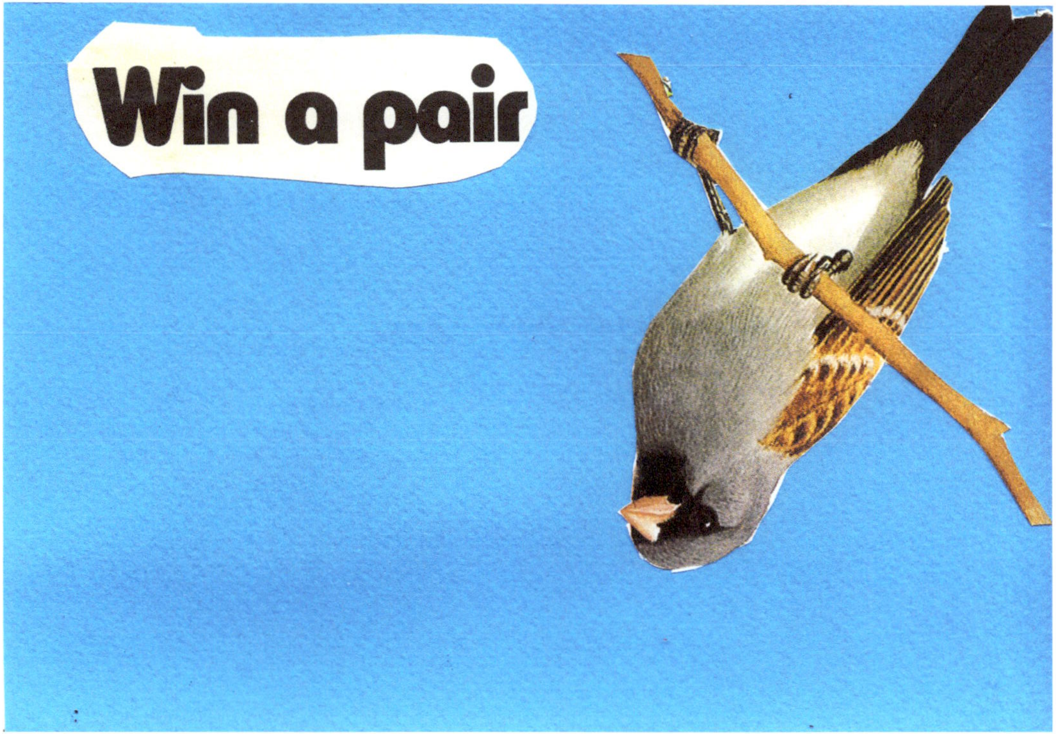
Win a pair

Wranglers vortex
Limestone landslide parade dog
Better run for it

No
Not either
Nothing

crepe
muscles
sly
freeze
fall
off
fone
fibs

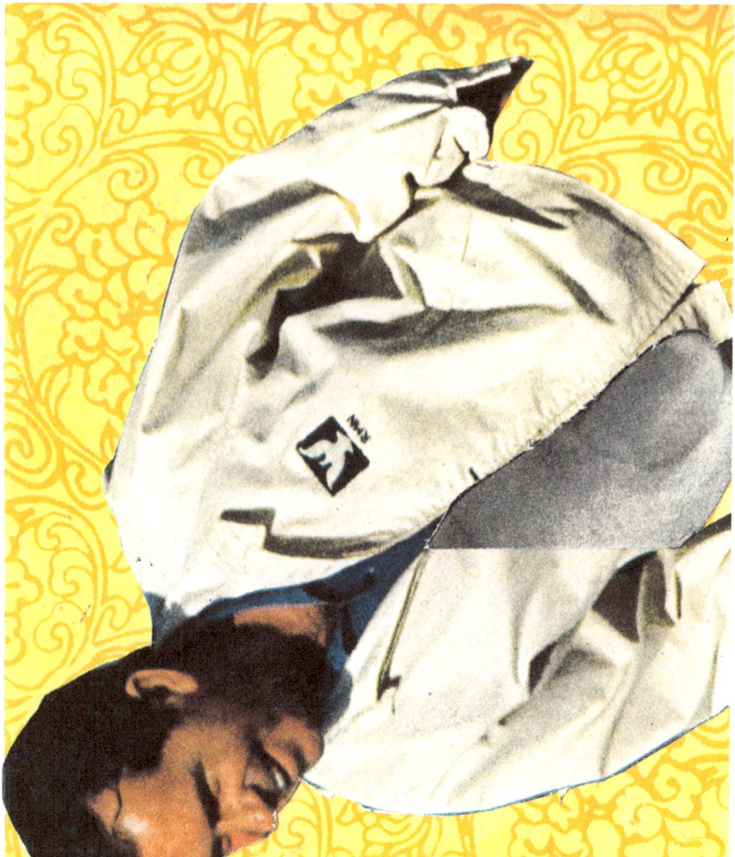

Where wildflowers stand taller
Than me if I can't feel you
I have nothing to say to you

No money
No money
No money

and
he
add
a
long
time
understand
govern
meant
touch

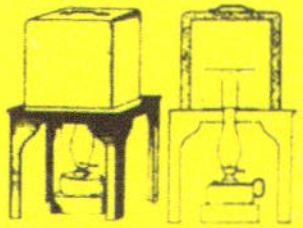

THE ATKINSON OVEN

THE "

WORKS

Over a year ago, MOTHER ann
sufficient" competition with the exp
directly below this box. The original ru
are in the first column on the facing
amended rules and regulations (plus an exp
the initial ones were changed) are in the s

That should bring all the Johnny-come
date except for the answers to two question
received over and over again from potential en
Yes, we've made the rules as general as possible
because we want to encourage completely

d introduced nationwide
d work, and enthusiasm
er invented. Remember,
lift Fisher Stoves if you

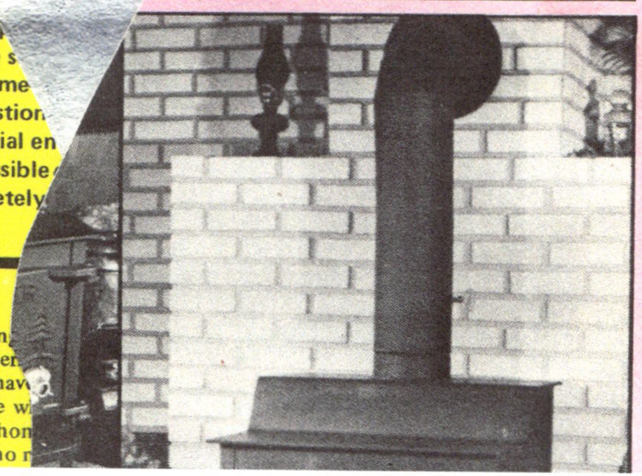

As you've surely noticed if you've done any eatin
of food has been going up. And not just in the super
Most of the stores that handle "organic" victuals hav
higher prices right along with the crowd. As have the w
deal to food co-ops . . . and the grain dealers from whon
freaks buy their supplies . . . and even the farmers who r

There's nothing more beautiful
Than two beautiful people
Making something beautiful together

Four season day
Folder lies empty
Talking points

moving
shit
around
mentally
at
least

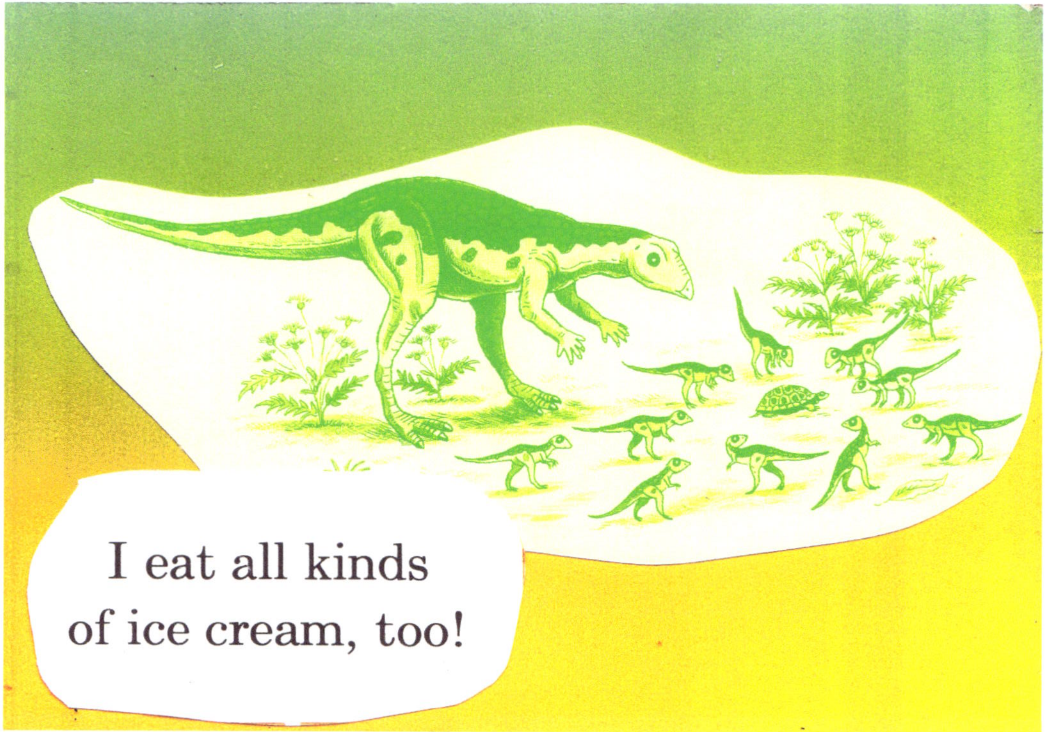
I eat all kinds
of ice cream, too!

Beachball tumbleweed
Across a city sleep
Citizens denizens

Kinda looks
Been and gone swatches
Watch mop

little
pit
of
everything

try
find
a
home

pass
find
ever
mold

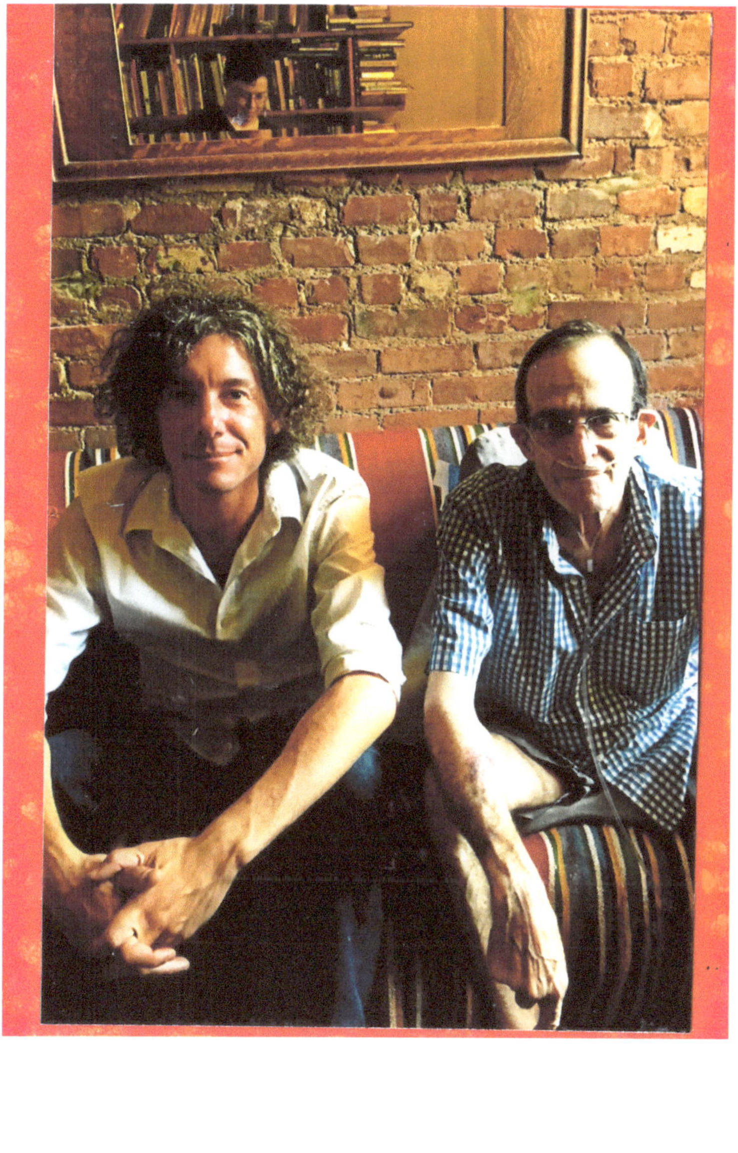

Tingle in the right arm
Chalkdust mouth
Think I'll pack it in and buy a pickup

Across USA
Gross out weather
So distressing about
this!

couple
deep
breaths
or
breathes

little
more
hop
on

couple
deep
breads

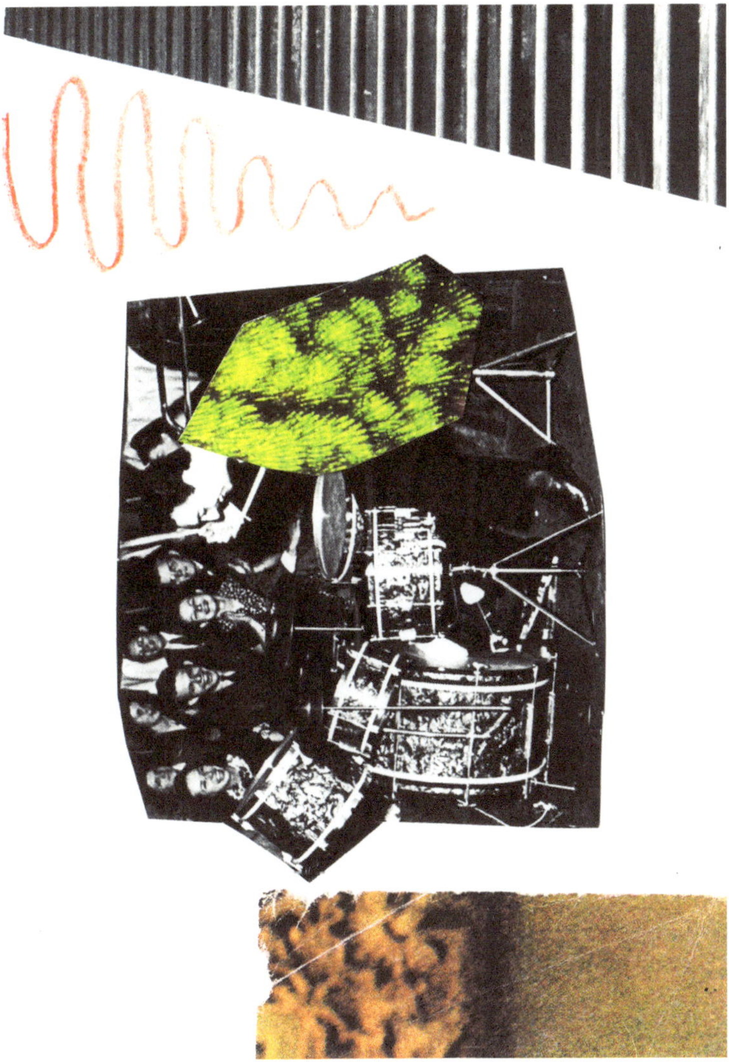

Wide awake and breathing hard
Green that is green that is green
Like there's no tomorrow resemble

Singer
A diff tune
Than I do

how
get
to
normal
get
to
know
you
patchy
streaky
light

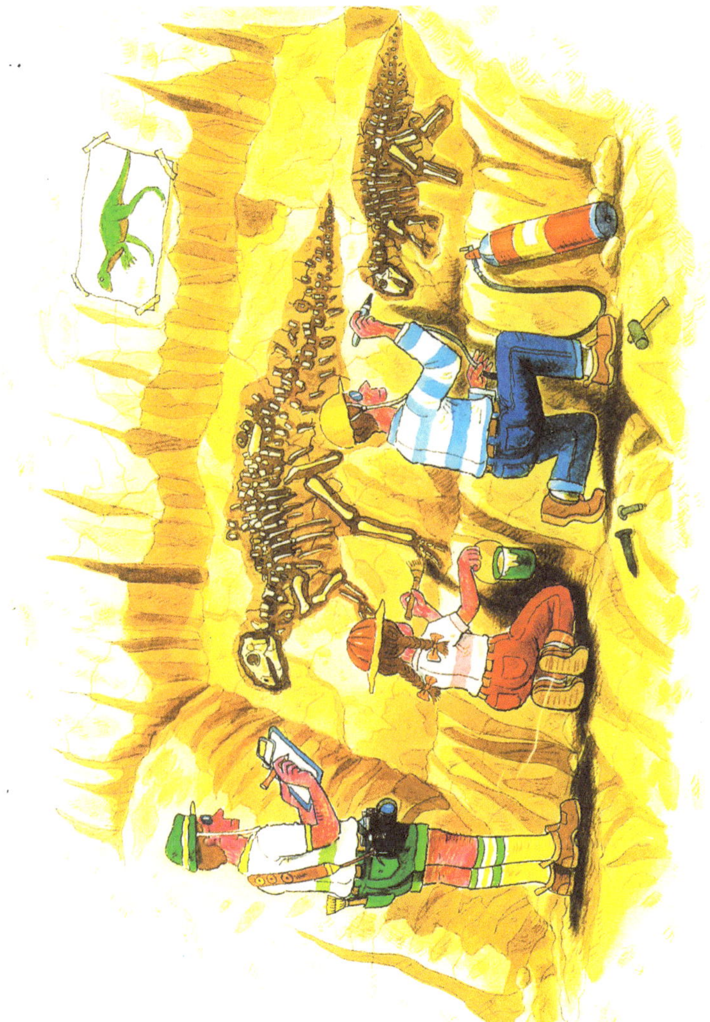

Comes a time
Birds of paradise
Comes a time

Calling all clouds
Country of origin
End user certificate

MOONPIE POMADE

there
you
go-go

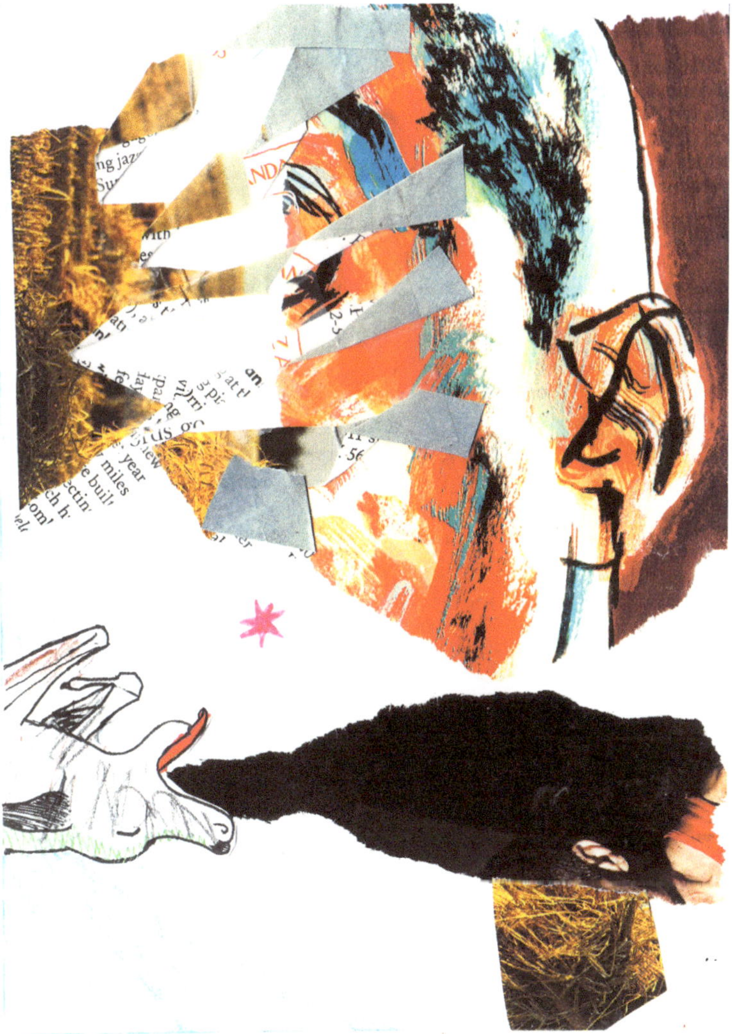

Pack it away no if ands or
But about in the
Tall grass tomorrow

5th in out
Anything on road
Let's go ~~places~~ faces

thanks
4
tow

U
Cannot
B
here

U
Know
U
Can

on... LIVING ON A SLOPE

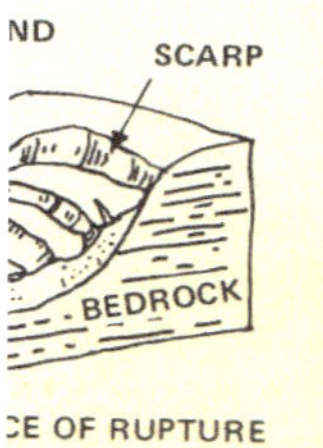

FIGURE 2

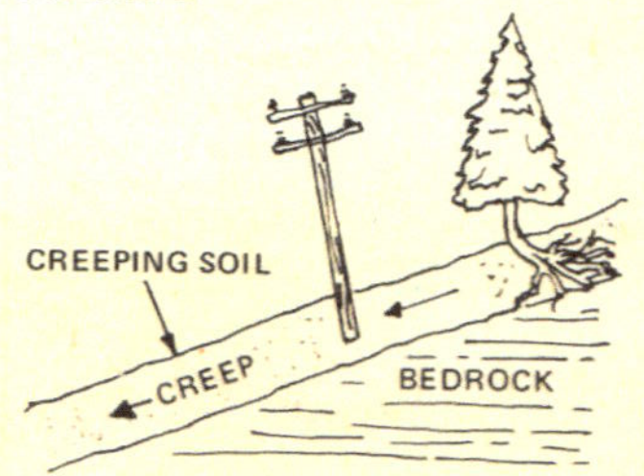

FIGURE 3

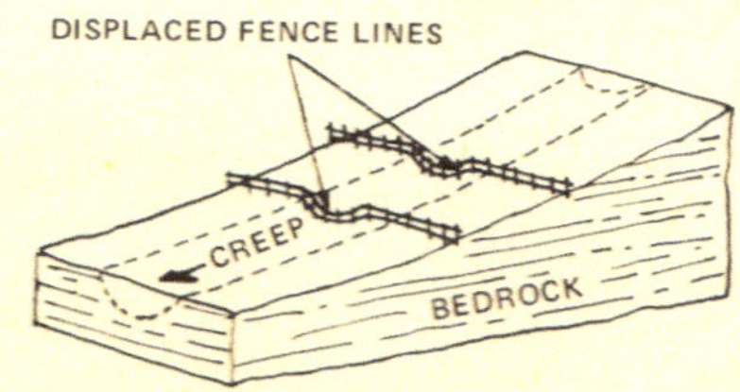

Everyday losers
Camel careening toward snatch
Batton down the hatch

Weather inventory
Today, do clouds
Today's done clouds

tie
toe
thru
piece
meal

Everything was groovy
On the magic sleighride
Then something happened

Happens yester
The at first
Hst later later

sit
2nd
person
down
drift

to
left
adrift

eyes
and
th'
ears

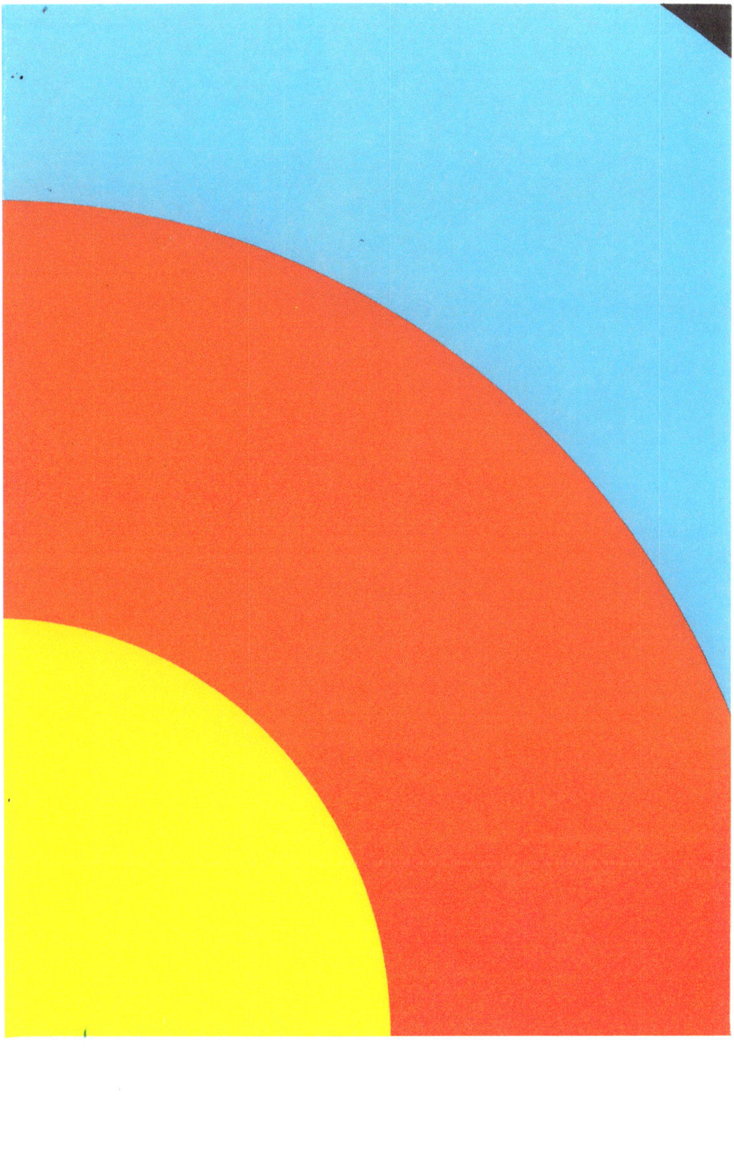

One step
And another
And another

Ah...
It...
Could work

on
the
double

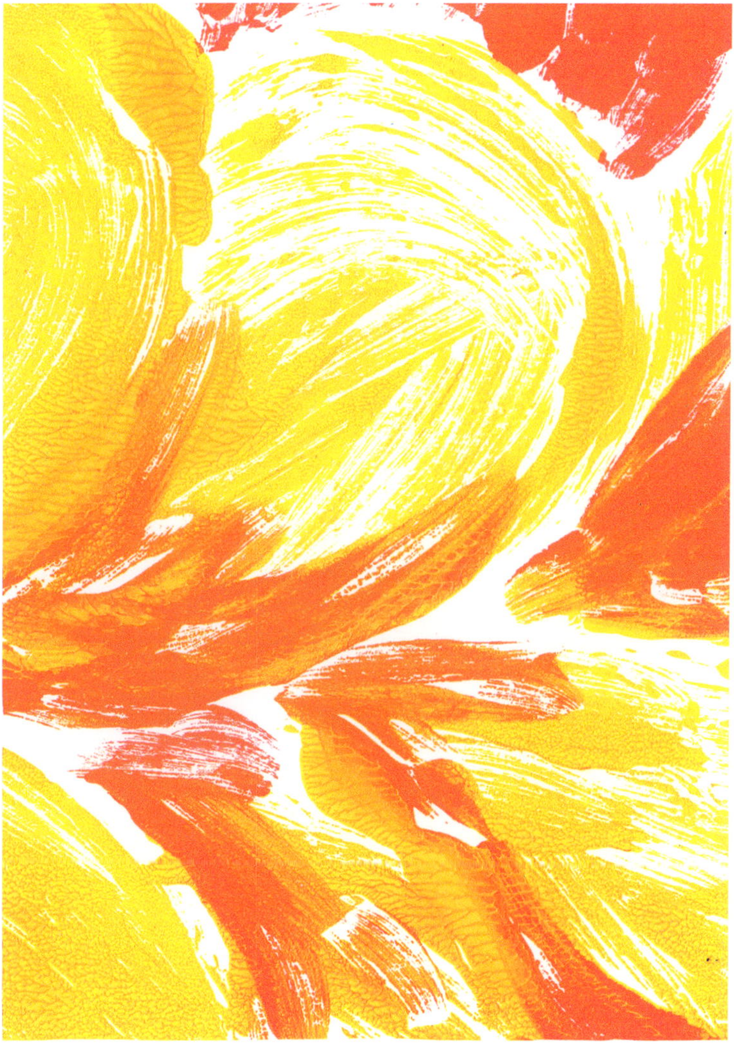

Time being
Hover light
Water over water

Nose on mind
Knife handwriting
Little kick

lettuce
head
roll
out
drive
way

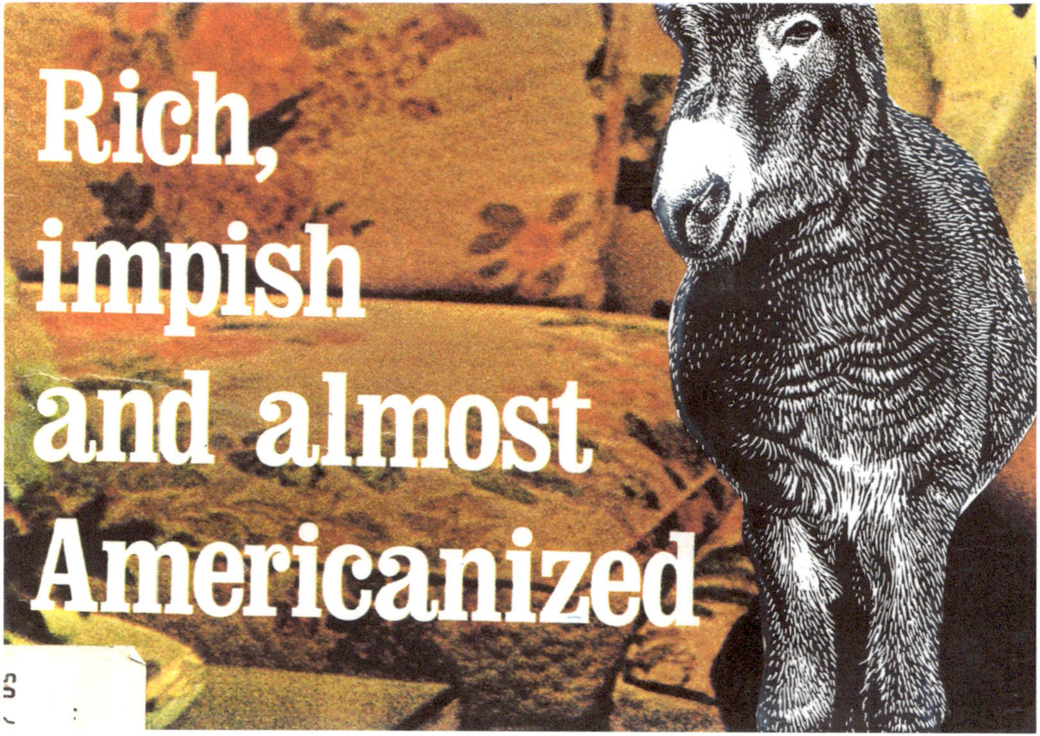
Rich,
impish
and almost
Americanized

My favorite picture of you
Watching the birds
A potato in the ~~alley~~ sky

Drive off in my hair
At foot of sea legs
Feel like family

you're
a
swell
bunch

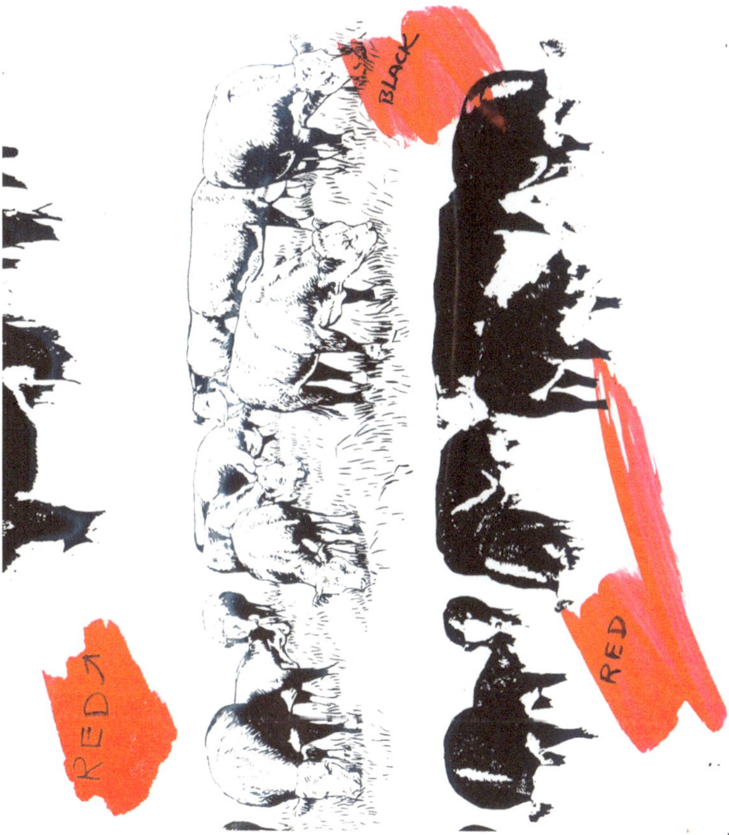
BLACK
RED
RED

Light change
The feeling that happens
In so many words

Little bird
Where is
Your little song

red
radish
come
over

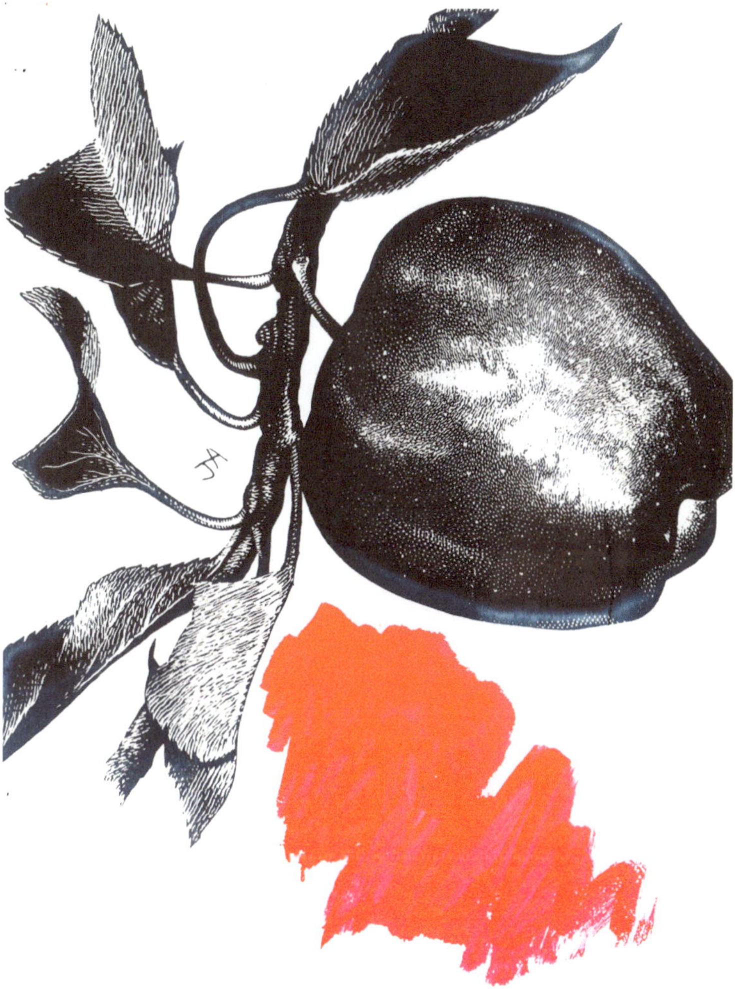

Camera clicks
Light both ends
Clouds cattle land

Sit around talking
Snowflake blossoms
Dicey

that
is

not
going
2
happen

so
many
things
in
motion

Change
pen tips

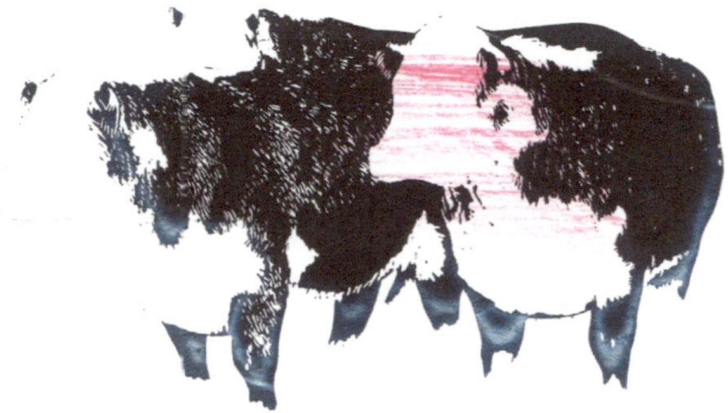
RED

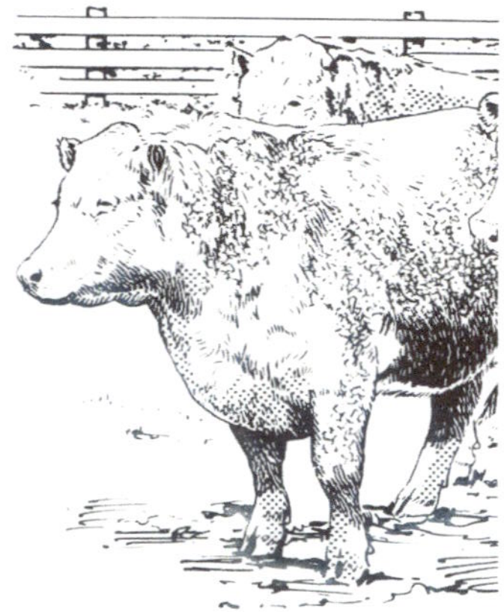
BLACK

Oui the people
It's personal
Another human

Bird jumping
And flapping
Be my beloved

can't
find
my
book

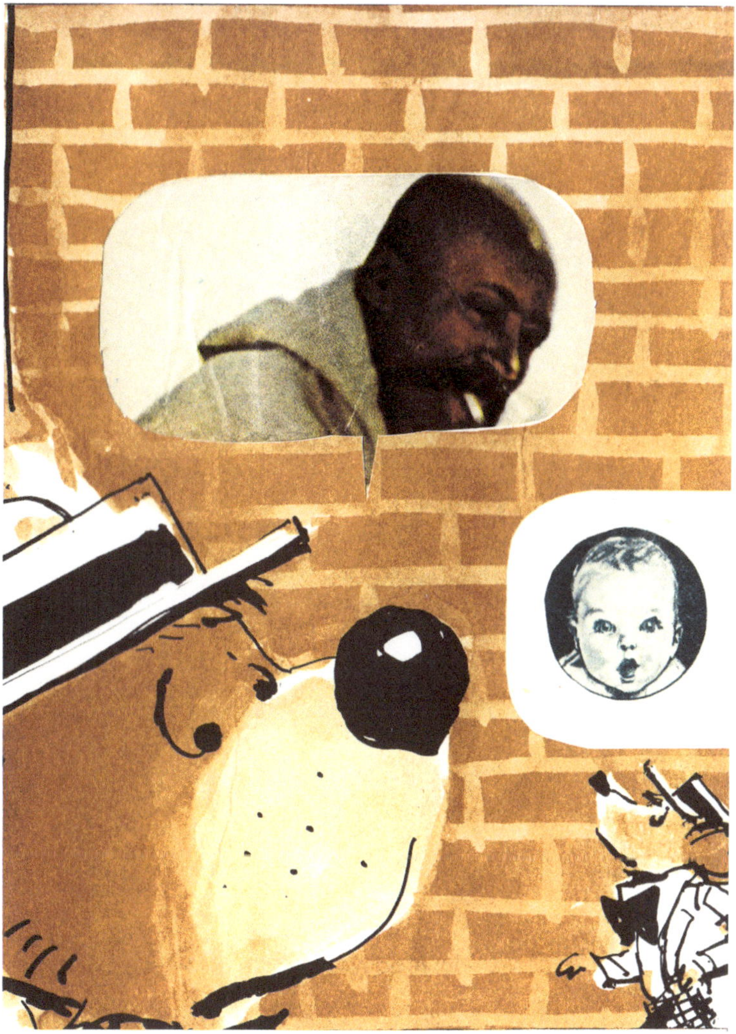

Misery scatters
About beauty
Take fire

Air across face
As eye they close
In air grammar

curl
hair
paté

one
of
the
best

other
shit
going
on

nice
music

head
shot

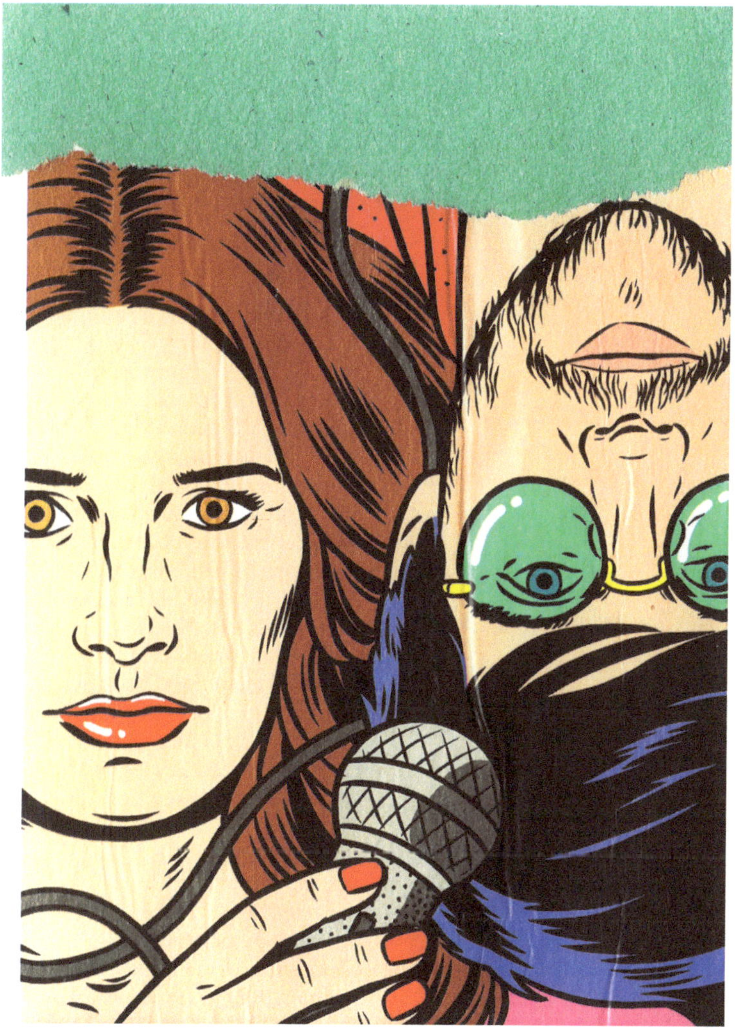

Heavy air
More barn
Stroke of genius

How this ends
The best restrooms
None of us

scream
into
night
light
showers
E
tart
trout

NONE OF US

Beam me a zinger
Beautiful beauty parlor
Best backup singers

•

Bud leaf shadows
Red brick w/ pompom
Window blotters

•

Sunset strip
Clams rubbernose
Loosey goosey placebo

•

Any simple animals walk by
They're people
The very people

•

Halcyon days scratch surface
So surmised is a sentence
Angels' braincells

•

Beyond Sound Bite Valley
Tundra-ing hoofs
Rush hour whistling snowflakes

•

Wranglers vortex
Limestone landslide parade dog
Better run for it

•

No
Not either
Nothing

•

Where wildflowers stand taller
Than me if I can't feel you
I have nothing to say to you

•

No money
No money
No money

•

There's nothing more beautiful
Than two beautiful people
Making something beautiful together

•

Four season day
Folder lies empty
Talking paints

•

Beachball tumbleweed
Across a city sleep
Citizens denizens

•

Kinda looks
Been and gone swatches
Watch mop

•

Tingle in the right arm
Chalkdust mouth
Think I'll pack it in and buy a pickup

•

Across USA
Cross out weather
So waitressing about this

•

Wide awake and breathing hard
Green that is green that is green
Like there's no tomorrow resemble

•

Singer
A diff tune
Thou T so

•

Comes a time
Birds of paradise
Comes a time

•

Calling all clouds
Country of origin
End user certificate

•

Pack it away no if ands or
But about in the
Tall grass tomorrow

•

5th in out
Anything on road
Let's go faces

•

Everyday losers
Camel careening toward snatch
Batten down the hatch

•

Weather inventory
Today, do clouds
Today's done clouds

•

Everything was groovy
On the magic sleighride
Then something happened

•

Happens yester
The at first
Hot later later

•

One step
And another
And another

•

Ah...
It...
Could work

•

Time being
Hover light
Water over water

•

Nose on mind
Knife handwriting
Little kick

•

My favorite picture of you
Watching the birds
A potato in the sky

•

Drive off in my hair
At foot of sea legs
Feel like family

•

Light change
The feeling that happens
In so many words

•

Little bird
Where is
Your little song

•

Camera clicks
Light both ends
Clouds cattle land

•

Sit around talking
Snowflake blossoms
Dicey

•

Oui the people
It's personal
Another human

•

Bird jumping
And flapping
Be my beloved

•

Misery scatters
About beauty
Take fire

•

Air across face
As eye they close
In on grammar

•

Heavy air
More barn
Stroke of genius

•

How this ends
The best restrooms
None of us

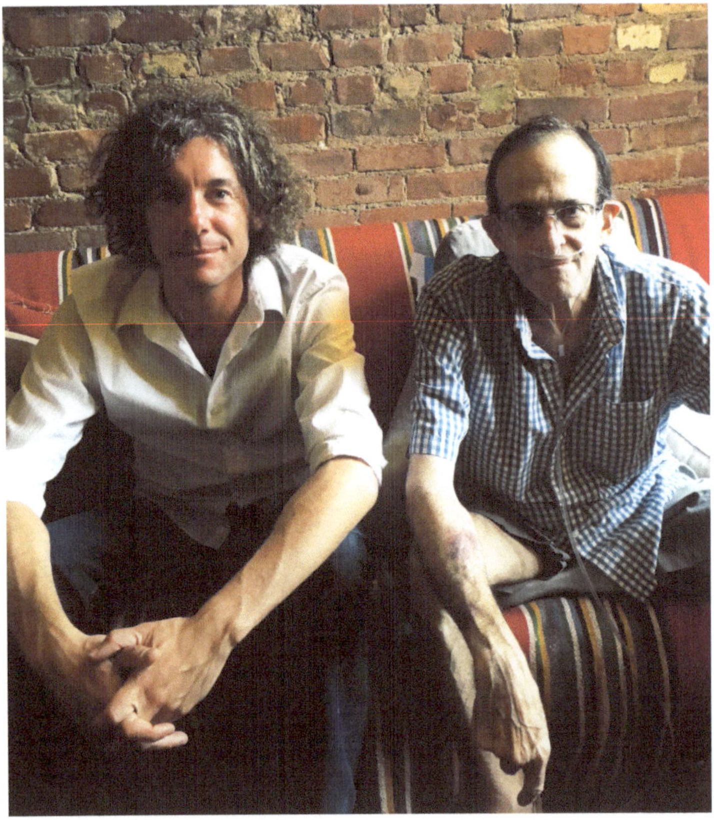

Photo by Abby Greenwald

Ted Greenwald (1942–2016) published over thirty collections of his poetry spanning more than fifty years, including *The Age of Reasons: Uncollected Poems, 1969–1982*, and a new edition of his early selected poems, *Common Sense*, both published by Wesleyan University Press.

Kyle Schlesinger is a poet, printer, and professor. Recent books include *A New Kind of Country* (Chax Press, 2020), *Color & Light* (Dusie, 2020), and *A Poetics of the Press* (Ugly Duckling, 2020). He resides in Austin, where he serves as the proprietor of Cuneiform Press.

www.ingramcontent.com/pod-product-compliance
Ingram Content Group UK Ltd.
Pitfield, Milton Keynes, MK11 3LW, UK
UKHW061026310726
14090UKWH00024B/423
* 9 7 8 0 9 9 8 9 2 9 3 3 0 *